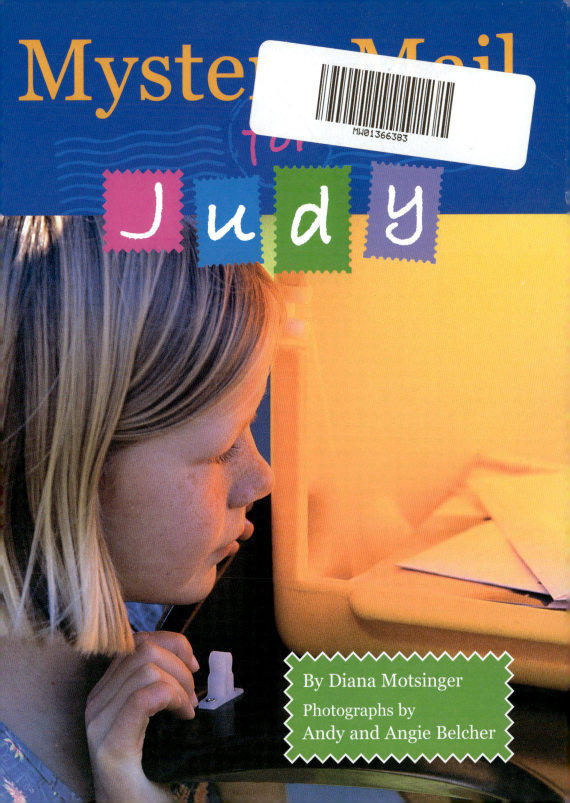

Mystery Mail for Judy

By Diana Motsinger

Photographs by Andy and Angie Belcher

Judy walked down the driveway to get the mail. Summer vacation was hot, long, and boring. It seemed as if all of her friends were away at camps, or off visiting fun-loving grandparents.

While her mom was at work, Judy had a babysitter who came over to keep her company. Unfortunately, the only thing Judy's babysitter wanted to do was read teen magazines. She was no fun at all. Lately, Judy had even started doing chores around the house without grumbling. At least it gave her something to do.

There was mail in the box. Judy sorted it as she walked back up the driveway: four bills for her mother, two brochures, and a letter. She turned the letter over. It was addressed to her, but who was it from?

July 12

Dear Judy,

It has come to our attention that you have been doing chores without grumbling. Your hard work is a big help to your mother.

In appreciation of all your efforts, we have enclosed our "Rewards of Summer" offer. This will familiarize you with our brochure, which you will receive in a few days. Simply select the gift that you would like. Return the enclosed order form, or e-mail your order. We will send the gift promptly.

Sincerely,
YDM Enterprises
(www.ydment.com)

Judy looked at the brochure. Across the top was a banner with *YDM Enterprises* written in red letters. Framed in the center was a picture of a sailboat on a mountain lake. Judy couldn't believe she had won something!

Judy carefully read the other side of the offer. Then she read the fine print at the bottom. Was this some kind of trick? At first, she felt like crying, and then she got mad. She went to her computer to type an e-mail.

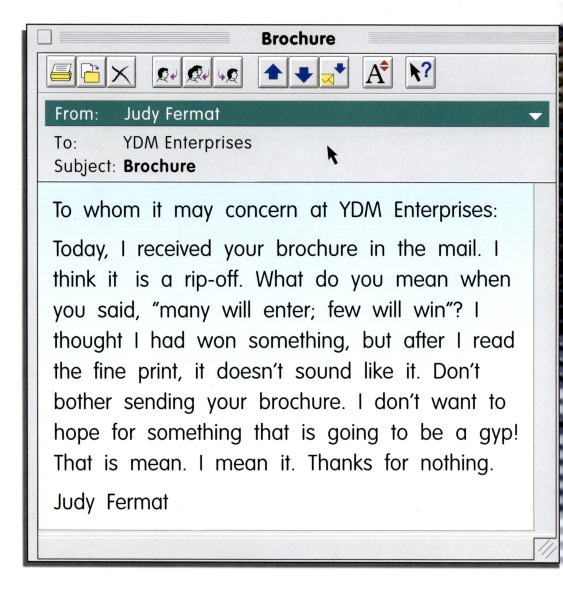

Judy really wanted to send the e-mail, but she didn't. Instead of hitting the "send" button, she deleted the message.

8

It was a trick her mother had taught her about the power of words and controlling her temper. She shoved the brochure and the letter under her bed and started to fold the laundry.

The following day, Judy checked the mail. She found a postcard from her best friend, Casey.

Dear Jude,

Hey, pal! How is it going? Camp is camp. We went rafting and I almost fell out. It has rained a lot. The food is just OK. I am starting to be homesick. You're so lucky to get to stay home! See you soon.

Your pal,
Casey

Judy Fermat
182 Oak Circle
Springfield
NE 68242

She also got a postcard from her second-best friend, Juliet.

Judy, Judy, Judy,

Ugh! I think I am going to die of boredom. I like to visit my grandparents, but they are a little crabby. They make me take naps! You're so lucky to stay at home. Rescue me and send me a letter, quick!

Love,
Juliet

Judy Fermat
182 Oak Circle
Springfield
NE 68242

Judy felt mixed up. She felt sorry for her friends and a little mad at herself for complaining about her summer at home. It never occurred to her that maybe she was better off right where she was. At least at night she could play cards with her mom, and she could read whenever she wanted to read. She wrote a long letter to Casey and another long letter to Juliet.

The next morning, when Judy went to the mailbox, she found a brochure waiting for her. She couldn't believe her eyes.

YDM Enterprises

Rewards of Summer

It's no trick, Judy. Here is what you've won! Take your pick!

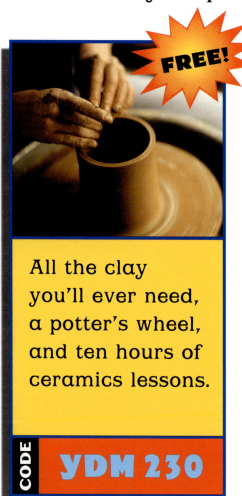

FREE!

All the clay you'll ever need, a potter's wheel, and ten hours of ceramics lessons.

CODE **YDM 230**

FREE!

Tickets to the symphony and six weeks of flute lessons. Shiny silver flute included.

CODE **YDM 231**

It took Judy hardly any time to make her choice. That night, Judy showed her choice to her mom, and together they e-mailed the order.

FREE!

Week-long getaway at Summer Lake. Sailboat and sailing lessons included.

CODE YDM 232

FREE!

Build your own library with a $200 gift certificate for the purchase of books. Oak bookcase included.

CODE YDM 233

15

The next day, Judy saw that there was a note on the refrigerator.

Dearest Judy,

Thank you for all your help around the house this summer. You've been such a sweetie. Your order has been processed, and we can take care of the details this weekend. We'll have fun! Thanks again.

Sincerely,
YDM (Your Dear Mother) Enterprises